Titles in the series

A SNOWY DAY
A STORMY DAY
A SUNNY DAY
A WINDY DAY

WHAT CAN I HEAR?
WHAT CAN I SEE?
WHAT CAN I TASTE?
WHAT CAN I TOUCH?

British Library Cataloguing in Publication Data

Butterworth, Christine
What can I taste? — (Giraffe books).
1. Taste — Juvenile literature
I. Title    II. Goffe, Toni    III. Series
612′.87    QP456

ISBN 0-340-42417-6

Text copyright © Christine Butterworth 1988
Illustrations copyright © Toni Goffe 1988

First published 1988

Published by Hodder and Stoughton Children's Books,
a division of Hodder and Stoughton Ltd,
Mill Road, Dunton Green, Sevenoaks, Kent TN13 2YJ

Printed in Italy

# WHAT CAN I TASTE?

Christine Butterworth

Illustrated by Toni Goffe

**HODDER AND STOUGHTON**
LONDON SYDNEY AUCKLAND TORONTO

Daddy and Joe are going to the park. They are taking Bess for a walk. Bess wags her tail and sniffs the air.

2

They have to cross a busy road.
There is a hot smell of petrol. A
lorry makes clouds of smoke.
Pooh! Joe holds his nose.

In the park, the air is fresh and cool. Joe breathes in deeply. Now he can smell earth and grass.

Joe sniffs as they pass the café.
'I can smell chips,' he says. The
smell makes Joe feel hungry.
'May I have some chips, Dad?'
asks Joe.

Joe loves chips. What is your favourite taste?

Cold chocolate ice cream?

Hot pizza with tomato and cheese?

Are there any tastes you don't like?

Try this game with a friend.
Cover her eyes with a scarf.
Then give her little bits of
different foods. Can she tell
what each bit is?

Look at your tongue in a mirror. Can you see little bumps all over it? These are called taste buds. They help you to taste your food.

You taste sweet things with
the tip of your tongue,

salty things
at the sides,

sour things
in the middle,

and bitter things at the back.

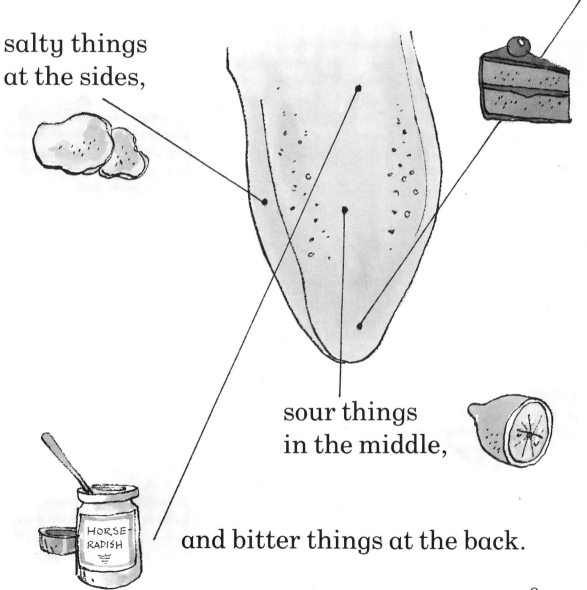

You need to smell food to taste it properly. If you do not like the smell of blue cheese, you will not like the taste.

Joe holds his nose if he has to take medicine. Then he can swallow it, without tasting it.

Does the smell of good food
make your mouth water?
This is the saliva coming.
Saliva mixes with the food
and helps you to swallow it.

The smell of food comes to you in the air you breathe. When you sniff, air is drawn into your nose. Sniff hard and the smell gets stronger.

Inside your nose, there are tiny hairs. These hairs trap any dust that you breathe in.

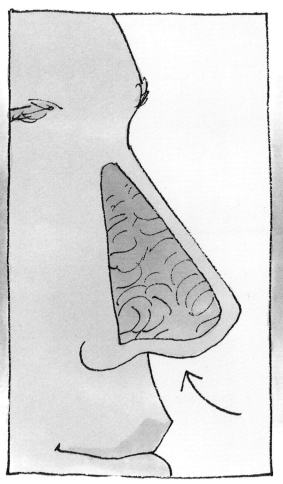
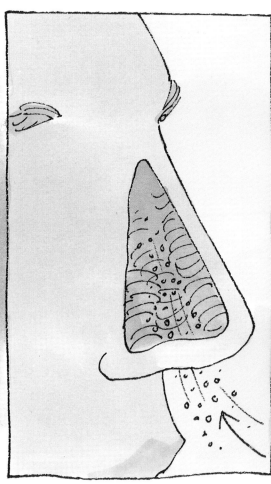

If a lot of dust gets into your nose, it tickles. You sneeze to get rid of the dust. Atishoo! Sneezing clears your nose.

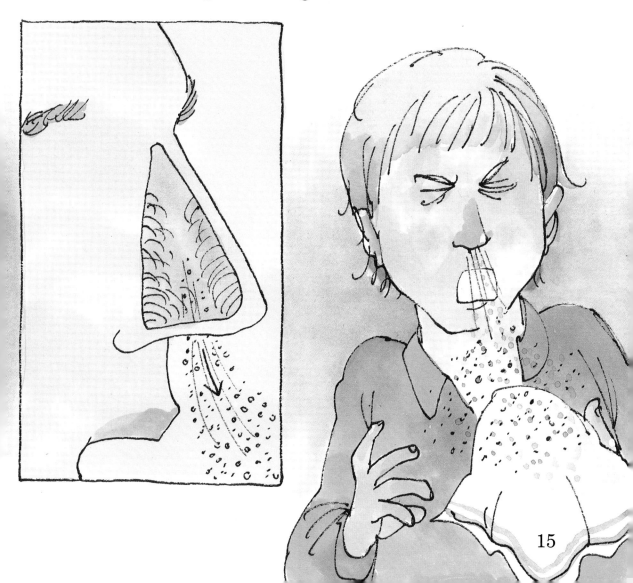

When you have a cold, your nose gets blocked. You must blow to clear it. Take care not to blow too hard.

If your nose is blocked, you cannot breathe through it. You cannot smell, and you cannot taste your food. Poor you!

Animals can smell things better than people. This farmer has lost some sheep under the snow. His sheepdog will find them by sniffing them out.

18

Bess can smell things that are
hidden, too. She smells a bone.
'Come out of the flowerbed,
Bess!'

Do you have a favourite smell?

A warm cake fresh from the oven?

Newly cut grass?

Your mum's perfume?

Pavements after rain?

Or is there another smell you
like better than any of these?

Joe is hungry again after the walk. As Joe and his dad get to the door, they smell something delicious.

It is a hot meaty smell. Mmm!
Joe's mouth begins to water.
It must be sausages, Joe's
favourite.
'Is it teatime, Mum?' he asks.

# tasting words

nasty smells

nice smells

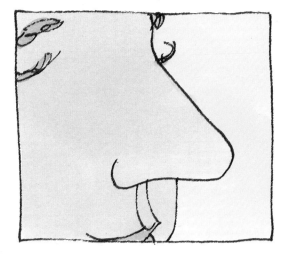

nose

sneeze

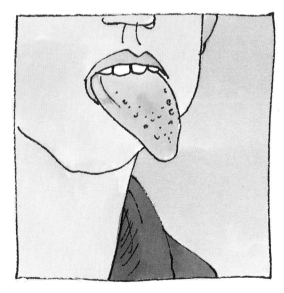

sniff

tongue